HERE

AND

NOW

For Liz

[signature]

4/22/14

ALSO BY STEPHEN DUNN

POETRY

What Goes On: Selected and New Poems 1995–2009

Everything Else in the World

The Insistence of Beauty

Local Visitations

Different Hours

Loosestrife

New and Selected Poems, 1974–1994

Landscape at the End of the Century

Between Angels

Local Time

Not Dancing

Work and Love

A Circus of Needs

Full of Lust and Good Usage

Looking for Holes in the Ceiling

PROSE

Walking Light: Essays and Memoirs

Riffs & Reciprocities

CHAPBOOKS

Five Impersonations

Winter at the Caspian Sea (with Lawrence Raab)

HERE

AND

NOW

poems

STEPHEN

DUNN

W. W. NORTON & COMPANY

NEW YORK · LONDON

For information about permission to reproduce selections from this book,
write to Permissions, W. W. Norton & Company, Inc.,
500 Fifth Avenue, New York, NY 10110

For information about special discounts for bulk purchases, please contact
W. W. Norton Special Sales at specialsales@wwnorton.com or 800-233-4830

Manufacturing by Courier Westford
Book design by JAM design
Production manager: Anna Oler

Library of Congress Cataloging-in-Publication Data

Dunn, Stephen, date.
Here and now : poems / Stephen Dunn. — 1st ed.
p. cm.
ISBN 978-0-393-08021-6 (hardcover)
I. Title.
PS3554.U49H47 2011
813'.54—dc22
                    2011001498

W. W. Norton & Company, Inc.
500 Fifth Avenue, New York, N.Y. 10110
www.wwnorton.com

W. W. Norton & Company Ltd.
Castle House, 75/76 Wells Street, London W1T 3QT

1234567890

. . . while we sleep here, we are awake elsewhere
and that in this way every man is two men.

—JORGE LUIS BORGES

. . . mere mortals in plain rooms.

—KATHLEEN LYNCH

CONTENTS

Acknowledgments 13

I

THE PURITAN AND THE WORLD 19

PROMISCUITY 23

LEAVING THE EMPTY ROOM 25

IMPOSTOR 27

THE GOOD NEWS 29

SCENES FROM THE ARGUMENTS 30

STONE SEEKING WARMTH 31

AFTER ECSTASY 32

THE GIRL IN THE NEON TANK TOP 33

THE WRITER OF NUDES 36

LOVE 38

WHY 40

HERE AND NOW 41

II

IF A CLOWN 45

DON'T DO THAT 47

TURNING YOURSELF INTO A WORK OF ART 49

THE TRAIL 51

PRUFROCK LATER 54

PERMISSIONS 56

LESSONS 58

BLIND DATE WITH THE MUSE 60

THE HOUSE ON THE HILL 62

BIRDS 64

III

THE CROWD AT THE GATES 67

THE WIND 68

THE REVOLT 70

LITTLE GOOD SONG 71

SHATTERINGS 72

THE MELANCHOLY OF THE
EXTRATERRESTRIALS 75

ONCE UPON 77

EVENINGS LIKE THIS 79

LANDSCAPE AND SOUL 82

IV

DISCREPANCIES 85

BAD 87

CONNUBIAL 89

THE IMAGINED 90

AROUND THE TIME OF THE MOON 91

ON THE PRAIRIE 93

LANDSCAPE WITH FRIENDS 95

A GREAT CELEBRATION 96

FINAL BOW 98

A HOUSE, A DESK, AND A CHAIR 99

ELSEWHERE 101

TO MY DOPPELGANGER 103

ACKNOWLEDGMENTS

The following poems have appeared in these journals:

AGNI: "Why"

The American Poetry Review: "Bad," "Birds," "Little Good Song,"
    "Promiscuity," "Prufrock Later," "The Writer of Nudes"

Boston Review: "After Esctasy," "Scenes from the Arguments"

The Cortland Review: "Blind Date with the Muse," "Here
    and Now," "Impostor," "Landscape and Soul," "To My
    Doppelganger"

Five Dials: "Permissions"

The Georgia Review: "The Good News," "The Girl in
    the Neon Tank Top," "The Puritan and the World,"
    "Landscape with Friends," "A Great Celebration"

Great River Review: "Shatterings"

Green Mountains Review: "The Crowd at the Gates,"
    "Around the Time of the Moon," "The Melancholy of the
    Extraterrestrials"

New Ohio Review: "Evenings Like This" (originally called
    "A Discreet Charm"), "Love"

The New Republic: "The Revolt," "Once Upon"

The New Yorker: "Discrepancies," "Don't Do That," "If a
    Clown," "The Imagined"

The Paris Review: "Leaving the Empty Room"

Poetry: "Connubial"

Poetry International: "Lessons," "The House on the Hill"

River Styx: "Stone Seeking Warmth"

Shenandoah: "A House, a Desk, and a Chair," "The Trail,"
    "Turning Yourself into a Work of Art"

"Turning Yourself into a Work of Art" was chosen for a 2010 Pushcart Prize.

Many thanks to Yaddo and the Macdowell Colony at which many of these poems got started.

HERE

AND

NOW

I

THE PURITAN AND THE WORLD

If I wanted more
of one thing, it was clear
I'd have to give up
something of another—
a third glass of wine, say,
would mean no dessert,
not even an espresso.
Look, I'm bountiful,
the world would whisper,
no need for you or anyone
to be so parsimonious,
I brim over
with phlox and hydrangea,
manatees and Holsteins,
the arbitrary, the disparate.

The world thought
I didn't understand it,
but I did, knew that to parse
was to narrow
and to narrow was to live
one good way.
Awash with desire
I also knew a little was plenty
and more than I deserved.
And because I was guilty
long before any verdict,
my dreams unspeakable,

I hunkered down
and buttoned up,
ready to give the world,
if I had to give it anything,
no more than
a closed-mouth kiss.

It was late afternoon,
late summer, a lone scud
streaking the sky,
and from my porch
I watched it drift away
from the world, this world
now cozying up to me,
claiming it, too, loves limits,
and offering shorelines
and riverbanks as proof,
the sweet pressures of death,
all the ripenings
that make possible the delicious.

But what I was hearing
was further evidence
that the world loved the all
of itself ad nauseam,
and would always lack—
when it came to truth telling—
the necessary cruelties

of exclusion.
The world got quiet; I thought
I might have quieted it.

Then I remembered
those cloud berries I picked
last summer in Nova Scotia.
They were bitter, truly awful,
and ever since
something in me
wanted their beautiful name
repudiated, the world
held accountable. Why couldn't
I just relax? Dusk now
was giving way to nightfall
and half-moon majesty,
and purple martins, in flight,
began to save us—
the good as well as the vile—
from an onslaught of mosquitos.

The world was showing off
again, and in the wake
of its grandeur I sensed
an honest complaint forming
in the shape of a question.
It would be about bitterness,
I was sure, and would want

to know how a man like me—
hairsplitter that I was,
corrector, ingrate—
hadn't developed a taste for it.

Which wouldn't be the first time
the world had turned on me.
I am my discriminations
(I would want to answer),
that's how I discover
what I love (*sometimes,*
I'd want to add). Meanwhile,
one of those rogue winds,
sudden and without motive,
came up from nowhere,
toppling the empty trash cans,
rolling them into the street.
I confess to a small pleasure
in returning them to the curb,
securing their lids,
while the world—smug
as a rose garden or as anything
that's never had to think about itself—
continued to spin and dazzle.

PROMISCUITY

When the neighbor's drapes are open,
I'm not *like* the kind of man
who refuses to put down his binoculars
so that their steamy, good time
can remain his as well. No,

I'm exactly that kind of man,
wary of anyone who'd turn away
mid-view, skedaddle off to a room
that overlooks, say, a pond.
I'm so tired of superior smiles.

Something I'm unaware of is likely
governing me, which doesn't excuse
these dark, bottom-feeding things
I tend to let rise into daylight.
I'll take discredit for all of them.

Nevertheless I wish to be true to life,
though not entirely to the one I live.
When in trouble I've been known
to give myself some wiggle room,
to revisit that once important sliver

of moon that slid across the Bay
to our table back when we were in love,
to even change our names. In the world
of feelings, aren't attractive opposites

always nearby?—dogwood blossoms,
for example, and the springtime puffery

of rhododendrons trumping the memory,
at least for a moment, of that heat
my binoculars brought close.
Life itself is promiscuous. It feels right
to place a few renegade details together,
let them cavort. A moment later,

it feels right to discipline them,
smack them into shape—the pink Cadillac
that motored by while I was eating macaroni
and cheese, the meteor that fell
at a terrible speed and dissolved into darkness,
that apology on the tip of my tongue.

LEAVING THE EMPTY ROOM

The door had a double lock,
and the joke was on me.
You might call it protection
against self, this joke,
and it wasn't very funny:
I kept the door locked
in order to think twice.
The room itself: knickknacks,
chairs and a couch,
the normal accoutrements.
And yet it was an empty room,
if you know what I mean.
I had a ticket in my head:
Anytime, it said, another joke.
How I wished I had a deadline
to leave the empty room,
or that the corridor outside
would show itself
to be a secret tunnel, perhaps
a winding path. Maybe I needed
a certain romance of departure
to kick in, as if I were waiting
for magic instead of courage,
or something else
I didn't have. No doubt
you're wondering if other people
inhabited the empty room.
Of course. What's true emptiness

without other people?
I thought twice many times.
But when I left, I can't say
I made a decision. I just followed
my body out the door,
one quick step after another,
even as the room started to fill
with what I'd been sure wasn't there.

IMPOSTOR

It sounds bad, you playing husband,
playing father, you playing the man
who starts to believe

the words on his business card,
putting on your suit in the morning
the way knights once put on their armor,

all day carrying a heaviness
that at first gets you down, yet soon
begins to feel normal, a chosen

weight, your very own masquerade.
It sounds bad, but you've tried hard
to successfully impersonate that man.

You've wanted act to become habit,
love replicated to be a definition of love,
though in fact you've been an impostor

of an impostor, often able to manufacture
authenticity when you've needed to,
then observing its effect. But consider

what used to sound good—someone
earnestly trying to be himself,
as if being oneself couldn't be hideous,

you and people you've known:
pigs in the slop, men in the throes
of discovering the joy in their malice.

THE GOOD NEWS

Looking back on it, what happens to us
often seems structured like a joke—the good news:
you've won first prize in the raffle
at the firehouse. The bad: you've been condemned

to a life of anticipating such happiness.
Hail to those who can tell us good news
and leave it at that—no niggling takebacks.
Your tormentors have been rounded up,

for example, and the ringleader hanged.
Or, she loves you, and is waiting at the cafe.
Periods after both. No exclamation points necessary.
But of course things are never that simple.

How can I tell you without hurting your feelings
that I don't like being called a gentleman?
Don't you know a scoundrel always wants his due?
The good news is I know who I am; that's the bad news, too.

SCENES FROM THE ARGUMENTS

You slam the door and walk out,
or you leave quietly,
pulsing the static air
with what you believe is a statement.
You come back with lilies
and her favorite steamed dumplings
as a way of saying you were wrong,
or you go to The Feel Sorry For Yourself
Bar down the street and put some dents
in your infrastructure, hurt yourself good.
You come back singing an old song,
or are mumbling when
she fetches you and drives you home.
Or you stay and fight it out,
or stay and let rough sex
calm you into mere resentment.
Or you turn on the television
as a way of being together
without having to be present.
Or you say nothing and carry it with you,
or you say nothing and let it go.
And your dreams become populated
with other people you could have loved,
and her dreams, too, are shameless
and equally full, aren't they? you ask,
even if she hasn't volunteered a thing.

STONE SEEKING WARMTH

Look, it's usually not a good idea
to think seriously about me.
I've been known to give others
a hard time. I've had wives and lovers—
trust that I know a little about trying
to remain whole while living
a divided life. I don't easily open up.
If you come to me, come to me
so warned. I am smooth and grayish.
It's possible my soul is made of schist.

But if you are not dissuaded by now,
well, my door is ajar. I don't care
if you're in collusion with the wind.
Come in, there's nothing here
but solitude and me. I wouldn't mind
being diminished one caress at a time.

Next morning
on the phone to her—
the all of it

reduced to words—
*How lovely the way
we redefined wrong.*

Yes, she agreed,
then slowly, in a hush,
*It went beyond
pleasure, beyond fun.*

They laughed
without gaiety.
I feel numb, he said,

and hung up to begin
what he'd later describe
as a long slide into himself.

Conversation with others
seemed like chatter.
Work felt like work.

He'd call her up
and say things like *Holy shit,*
which she understood
to be accurate.

THE GIRL IN THE NEON TANK TOP

She sought the allure of a look
that would separate her
from the conventional, the all.
In this she was like most girls
except she was precocious
and believed appearance
is a kind of truth, and that a truth
lasts only so long—is, in fact,
always secretly expecting
to be disrobed. She was,
in other words, a philosopher
of the charged sartorial moment,
and had intuited the importance
of dressing in order to be found,
and often conjured
being ravished by a boy
with taste so fine he'd strip away
her disguises one tenderness
at a time. Of course she was
only a teenage philosopher,
unschooled in the way experience
confounds one's ideas.
Dressed just right or perfectly
wrong, say, in her neon tank top
and precisely tattered jeans,
she'd stroll one of those
well-lit boulevards of hope,
only to be ignored by men

afraid of the law, or catcalled
by boys who feared a girl
who seemed to promise
exactly what they had dreamed.
How long most days were,
but how interesting to be
the sole inhabitant of herself,
her parents forever at work,
and no girlfriends, except Janet,
equally good at precalc.
The summer was almost over
when at an ice-cream stand
a shy, nice boy asked her name.
She lamented she was wearing
a plain white halter
and nothing-to-speak-of shorts,
but she liked the way he looked,
and found herself formulating
what she believed
to be a new system of thought—
one face for the world,
another for the party you want
to be yours. It wasn't new, of course,
and she wouldn't know for years
it also was insufficient,
that she'd need many more faces
than two if she were to fully live,

not to mention at least one
black dress adaptable to whim
and the lay of the land.

When I ask women of various shapes and ages
to pose, it seems to help that I'm short
and slight of build, and that my voice
has a lot of boy in it. So when I say,
Would you like to be described? very few
take umbrage, though many do walk away.
I tell them that every body has a grammar,
and I'm looking for that grammar, and when
I compose I'm not seeking excitement—
in fact, no offense, I try to be a little bored.
Still, some women about to be turned into words
can't relax. They don't know that I love sweat
and goose bumps as much as any lovely curve,
that for me the body, like landscape,
can do no wrong; my eye will just find
what it needs. But soon, I've learned,
it's best to prepare them for truths
beneath the truths I've told. I say,
Don't expect to see yourself as other
than I see you. Sometimes I'll suffuse you
in prose so dark you'll simply be evidence
of a mood. Or I'll drape you in rueful shadows,
or devote a paragraph to the angel
I see behind that scar or that bruise.
Nevertheless, the girl who posed last week
didn't like the way I'd abstracted her—
an arm where her head should be, breasts
coming out of her eyes. How, she asked,

could I have written, *She was like*
a Duchamp without even a staircase.
I chose not to say. How could I tell her
I'd shown her in the best possible light.

LOVE

Found dead in an alley
of words: *awesome,*
no hope for it, and *share,*
which must have fallen
trying to get by on its own,
and near the trash cans,
almost totally exhausted,
the barely breathing *cool.*

But there's *love*
among the disposables,
waiting, as ever,
to be lifted
into consequence.

And here comes a forager
looking for anything
that might get him
through another night.
Love's right in front
of him, his if he wants it.

In the air
the ashy smell of cliches,
the stink of obsolescence.
He's leaning love's way.

All the words are watching,
even the dead ones. It's as if
what he does next
could be the equivalent
of restoring *awe* to awesome—

that *love,* if chosen,
might be given back to love,
made new again.

But the man is just a man
out for easy pickings.
Or has he just remembered
how, early on, love
always feels original?

Let us forgive him
if he keeps on foraging.

Because you can be sure a part of yourself is always missing
and if directly pursued cannot be found

Because this morning you woke to this question: for the sake
of justice, how many people would I deceive?

Because you believe most good lessons are just a hunger away
from being unlearned

Because the oboe is the instrument to which other instruments
are tuned, and there's not an oboe in sight

Because there's little sympathy for the achievements of forgery
or your desire to have more than one of most things

Because it seems the angels who once whispered only to you
are indiscriminate agents of the wind

Because when it comes to love, the word *forever* has so often
made you a liar, and here you go again

HERE AND NOW

for Barbara

There are words
I've had to save myself from,
like My Lord and Blessed Mother,
words I said and never meant,
though I admit a part of me misses
the ornamental stateliness
of High Mass, that smell

of incense. Heaven did exist,
I discovered, but was reciprocal
and momentary, like lust
felt at exactly the same time—
two mortals, say, on a resilient bed,
making a small case for themselves.

You and I became the words
I'd say before I'd lay me down to sleep,
and again when I'd wake—wishful
words, no belief in them yet.
It seemed you'd been put on earth

to distract me
from what was doctrinal and dry.
Electricity may start things,
but if they're to last
I've come to understand
a steady, low-voltage hum

of affection
must be arrived at. How else to offset
the occasional slide
into neglect and ill temper?
I learned, in time, to let heaven
go its mythy way, to never again

be a supplicant
of any single idea. For you and me
it's *here and now* from here on in.
Nothing can save us, nor do we wish
to be saved.

Let night come
with its austere grandeur,
ancient superstitions and fears.
It can do us no harm.
We'll put some music on,
open the curtains, let things darken
as they will.

II

If a clown came out of the woods,
a standard-looking clown with oversized
polka-dot clothes, floppy shoes,
a red, bulbous nose, and you saw him
on the edge of your property,
there'd be nothing funny about that,
would there? A bear might be preferable,
especially if black and berry-driven.
And if this clown began waving his hands
with those big, white gloves
that clowns wear, and you realized
he wanted your attention, had something
apparently urgent to tell you,
would you pivot and run from him,
or stay put, as my friend did, who seemed
to understand here was a clown
who didn't know where he was,
a clown without a context.
What could be sadder, my friend thought,
than a clown in need of a context?
If then the clown said to you
that he was on his way to a kid's
birthday party, his car had broken down,
and he needed a ride, would you give
him one? Or would the connection
between the comic and the appalling,
as it pertained to clowns, be suddenly so clear
that you'd be paralyzed by it?

And if you were the clown, and my friend
hesitated, as he did, would you make
a sad face, and with an enormous finger
wipe away an imaginary tear? How far
would you trust your art? I can tell you
it worked. Most of the guests had gone
when my friend and the clown drove up,
and the family was angry. But the clown
twisted a balloon into the shape of a bird
and gave it to the kid, who smiled,
letting it rise to the ceiling. If you were the kid,
the birthday boy, what from then on
would be your relationship with disappointment?
With joy? Whom would you blame or extol?

DON'T DO THAT

It was bring-your-own if you wanted anything
hard, so I brought Johnnie Walker Red
along with some resentment I'd held in
for a few weeks, which was not helped
by the sight of little nameless things
pierced with toothpicks on the tables,
or by talk that promised to be nothing
if not small. But I'd consented to come,
and I knew in what part of the house
their animals would be sequestered,
whose company I loved. What else can I say,

except that old retainer of slights and wrongs,
that bad boy I hadn't quite outgrown—
I'd brought him along, too. I was out
to cultivate a mood. My hosts greeted me,
but did not ask about my soul, which was when
I was invited by Johnnie Walker Red
to find the right kind of glass, and pour.
I toasted the air. I said hello to the wall,
then walked past a group of women
dressed to be seen, undressing them
one by one, and went up the stairs to where

the Rottweilers were, Rosie and Tom,
and got down with them on all fours.
They licked the face I offered them,
and I proceeded to slick back my hair

with their saliva, and before long
I felt like a wild thing, ready to mess up
the party, scarf the hors d'oeuvres.
But the dogs said, No, don't do that,
calm down, after a while they open the door
and let you out, they pet your head, and everything
you might have held against them is gone,
and you're good friends again. Stay, they said.

Turning Yourself into a Work of Art

If you find your left hand gesturing, involuntarily,
in the direction of the moon, it may be time
to handcuff your right to something cast iron,
impossible to move. Balance is everything,

or almost everything, if you want to be
a work of art. All too soon you'll be old,
and no amount of wisdom
will compensate for that wobble and drool.

You taste like a grape, a woman once said,
after she spit out something essentially yours.
Whether a detail like that should be included
in an attempt to turn yourself into a work of art

                    is questionable.

But you'd like to think it a formal issue,
the way the straps of a purse, that memorable slash,
accentuated the breasts of that same woman,
guiding your eyes in a manner she intended.

        A work of art

always is in danger of wanting more
than it can give itself permission to have.
All your life, haven't you reached
for what hasn't yet been offered? Before you die

you think you must risk some falling apart
of whoever you are, your heart loose
and banging against its rib cage—
another formal issue. You have in mind a painting

in which a solitary green shoe in the forefront
exists only because that dagger with a jade handle
on the night table needed an aesthetic companion.
In other words, you wish to be an arrangement,

and you wish to be the arranger.

Can there ever be enough distance from yourself
to get yourself right? It's hard, and should be,
to become a work of art. Maybe the trick is
to avert your gaze, look a little sideways

as an astronomer does.

That's how a faint star becomes visible—
just a glimpse at first, then the long adventure
of saying what exactly it is that shines
behind so much of its own smoke and gas.

THE TRAIL

Begin Here, the trail sign said,
as if we would have begun at the end
or parachuted down into the middle.
It's the discrepancies and absurdities
that always have cheered us,
like desiring a balcony overlooking
a turbulent sea, and every summer
renting a shack near a pond.

In fact, we did what the sign said
to do, and soon there were arrows,
color-coded, pointing toward
different trails, and others—
our favorite arrows—
which essentially advised us
to remain steady and true.

Along the way, we heard
the sound of bullfrogs
and some rustling in the underbrush.
There was birdsong, and now
and then we were visited
by what seemed like
little thunderclaps of thought,
which failed to startle us

into any fine distinctions
between insight and nonsense,
beginning and end. But perhaps
that was too much to expect.
On the trail, we just needed
to follow the arrows. Off the trail,

of course, we would have worried
about such unquestioning obedience,
might have seen in it the lassitude,
the cowardice, that opens the door
for something tyrannical.

But on the trail we trusted the signs
had our interests at heart,
felt no need to cut a rebellious swath
through the tall reeds, or to invent
a strange impediment—some troll
or seldom invoked tautology—
that must be circumvented.

On the trail or off the trail,
we knew an awfulness surrounded us,
yet believed an occasional hurrah
was never very far away.
But we weren't stupid,
as that insulting, large-lettered

End Of Trail sign suggested we were.
Just where did they think
we thought we had come to.

Let us not look back then at that time
of despair and oddities in the sky
with any intention of prettying it up.
Mine was no heroic submission to the gods,
but a terrible awkwardness before bare arms
and assured voices of women whose necklaces
dipped farther down than my eyes had gone.
But let us revisit the years thereafter—
and please hear me out
now that so much has calmed—
when sometimes I'd dare to extend
an argument, kiss a proffered hand,
swig some bourbon even in the afternoon.
No, I was never brave, but learned to seek
company that would be company—men
like me, and a few unperfumed girls
who didn't make me feel I was scuttling
across some ocean floor. Slim women of Soho,
speaking in hushed tones, all dressed in black—
I will not again climb their lonely stairs.
But I digress. Come, I want you to meet
the woman who gave me a peach
and licked the juice as it slid down my chin,
the woman I married, waiting for us now
in the park. And let me take you
to the bank where I rose from clerk
to manager, where still I work, then to
a few of those no longer deserted streets

with my dog Sadie on her leash.
Oh I know how large the spaces are
between reach and grasp, and how hard it is
to escape oneself, but I'd like you to believe
I've learned to sing a different song.

The veil of weather, the hopeful smell
of just-cut grass, the who-knows-what
that goes on behind closed doors—

all commingle, become strange companions,
if we can make a place for them.

The ocean, its undulations
and its calm, the variety of what it hides,
the ways it crashes and recedes,

is clearly one big thing,

and those unaffordable, grand vistas
at the end of cliffs, and the poor bastard
on his porch peeling an orange

could meet in some macrosphere,
if such a place can be made.

Blueberries for the picking
in a neighbor's field, ten cents a box,
a snake sunning itself on a rock—

"the power of the mind
over the possibilities of things,"

permitting even the impermissible,
yet in the gray, shimmery air
of our best intentions, sometimes

the easy lie, the forced resemblance.

LESSONS

One summer when I was young
and open to influence and desperate
to be other than I was,
That is no country for old men
cadenced everything I said.
I could be speaking about
my mother's tea cup collection
or Kurosawa's latest film, yet
I couldn't stop hearing
that assertive, modulated claim.
Meanwhile, almost everywhere,
the sexual revolution had begun—
closet doors opening,
women fond of cleavage
at odds with women burning bras,
men saying, May I?
and girls not waiting to be asked.
Why not favor all of it, I thought,
or at least let me in far enough
to decide? My experience
up to that point was little
more than little more. I wondered
if Yeats had found himself
similarly fascinated and disoriented.
After all, there was Maud,
her passionate resistance,
her devotion to a cause—a woman
unlike any he'd known.

If I can't have everything,
the romantic in him must have thought,
let me settle for the unattainable.
It took me years to learn life isn't kind
to those with obsessions,
and yet the self *selves;* with time,
even Yeats would turn to troubles
larger than just his own.
After that summer, I subdued
his singular voice with many voices,
some expansive, some clipped
and hesitant, often unmelodious,
and free verse like free love
began to seek only what might
constrain and tightly hold it.
Soon, more than I knew
how to accommodate—
tiger lilies, jackhammers, mudslides,
all the stuff of the palpable world—
seemed to want something from me.
I had to learn ways to exclude.
Meanwhile the great criminals
walked right in, left with the jewels.

Well, not exactly blind; I knew of her.
I was the needy unknown, worried
about appearance, and what, if anything,
she'd see beneath it. And, desperate
as this sounds, it was I who fixed myself up—

I didn't mind being middleman
to the man I longed to be. "Yes," she agreed,
then, "I hope you're not the jealous type."
I lied, and she named the time and place,
told me there'd be others, ever and always.

The door was open. And there we all were—
men and women, empty handed
and dressed down—each of us hoping
to please by voice, by tone. In her big chair
she welcomed or frowned, and one man

she gently touched, as if to say, "Don't
despair, it will be delivered soon."
Even as I hated him, I took heart.
She was the plainest woman I'd ever seen.
I wanted to make her up, but all arrangements

seemed hers—I found myself unable
to move. "You look lonely," she said,
"a little lost, the kind of man
who writes deathly poems about himself.
Sensitive, too," she added, and laughed.

Thus began the evening the Muse,
that lifelong tease, first spoke to me.
"If you want to be any good
you must visit me every day," she said.
And then, "I'm hardly ever home."

THE HOUSE ON THE HILL

An attention to detail, many believed,
was the way in, the tao of getting
from sea level to the large house
at the end of the road, atop the hill.

Too much telltale noise if you drove,
so you'd walk, noting rosebush
and dragonfly and ugly slug—
nothing unworthy of your gaze.

You might see a schooner
offshore with white sails unfurled,
and, high above, perhaps a plane
gliding motorless over the entire scene.

You observed and named, and at the end
of what you saw might come an idea,
something to help you avoid or engage
whatever was inside. But you always felt

in danger of becoming humorless, overly
purposeful, a prisoner of that one idea.
You'd will yourself then to look down,
and the simplest stone you'd come upon

would turn, say, into an emerald
illuminating a path. Or you'd extract
from the blackberries an invisible stain,
your passport, and soon, from out of the fog,

a large, welcoming house would emerge
made out of invention and surprise.
No things without ideas! you'd shout,
and the doors would open,

and the echoes would cascade down
to the valleys and the faraway towns.
In your dreams, of course. In real time,
the weather wouldn't be right, or ghosts

disguised as dogs would be blocking the gate.
Still, the long climb itself was what
each day you woke to plan and think about.
It simply was what you did,

you didn't have a choice, even if
your words again and again were met
by silence, or those doors opened
to a world you couldn't abide.

At breakfast this morning I told a woman
named Dalit that right outside my window
a bird had been singing her name.
No doubt it meant I'd been thinking of her,
and she seemed pleased. I suppose the bird
could have been singing Larry,
had I been thinking of him. But, no,
I was sure it kept repeating *Da-lit, Da-lit.*
Years ago I resolved to try hard
not to become like the whip-poor-will,
its beautiful lilt turning monotonous
as it kept calling out its own name.
I'd try to be like a mockingbird instead,
the one that included in its repertoire
many birds as well as the meow of my cat.
At dinner last night some of us were listing
books that we hate. I couldn't think of any,
so I made one up. Dalit wasn't present.
Da-lit, Da-lit. A mockingbird never stops
including, though often it may seem
unoriginal, indiscriminate, inordinately
pleased with itself. But why shouldn't it?
Imagine how surprise turns into delight
as each time it sings it hears another voice.
After many mornings, it is all of its voices.
What fascinates? How do we know
what we love? I trespass, steal, accumulate,
I do what the mockingbird does.

III

The Crowd at the Gates

The crowd had gathered by the gates.
Like most crowds, it was more shifty
than intelligent, on the verge
of dangerous. At times it undulated
like gelatin, at others its movements
were barely perceptible, as if it were
waiting for some kind of permission.
A crowd, the gates knew, was a tsunami
in the making. Which is why the gates
were needed—big, stolid, iron gates
clear about their mission. The crowd
had gathered by them, and the gates
feared someone would make a speech.
The gates always feared the articulate
appeal to a collective deprivation.
The gates had experience. They knew
that after such speeches, crowds lack
a sense of humor, which can diffuse
misery, make a crowd break up.
Behind the gates was the stronghold,
in which the deciders made their decisions.
The gates would try to protect them,
as ever. The crowd was getting larger,
swaying now. Someone began to speak,
and for a moment the gates wondered:
If it were possible for us to be moved,
might we, too, be outraged, want to open
ourselves wide, and say, *Get them!*

THE WIND

Tomorrow, our weatherman said,
the wind would hardly exist in Kansas
yet would arrive full throttle in Maryland,
and with his pointer showed us
his version of something beautiful—
the arc and dip of the jet stream.

I must confess a part of me wished
he'd also speak of tedium
and long afternoons of nothingness,
but finally he was a Doppler man, dour,
only as smart as his equipment.
Next day the wind did come full throttle,

and branches fell, and I was careful
not to die. A calm followed, then
the mail, and in it an aerogramme
from a friend in a land so tumultuous
tedium for him would be a luxury,
already the stuff of nostalgia.

It was a disturbing letter, and I imagined
a country without a weatherman,
and the wind, therefore, without anyone
to speak for it, or worse—that the wind
belonged to the rulers now,

and everyone was forbidden to speak
of what they remembered—
those big, generous winds
that once had mussed their hair
and felt so good against their faces.

Picture a certain banker's house and its crawl space,
then imagine a circumstance in which he has to crawl.
If you want to take part, imagine rats' nests
and a leaking pipe, and all the plumbers in the world
tired of shit, not answering their phones. For I have
come to my banker's house, already having unscrewed
what down below was screwed tight. I've rung his bell,
and have been made to wait in the garden
and take off my shoes. Time used to be money.
Now it's an invisible hand slapping you in the face.
He has told me, in so many words, my kind
of industriousness is cancelled by his kind of dream.
He wrote a letter explaining this, the fallout
from the windfall, the gobble and the gobbledegook,
and four or five reasons why all necessity is his.
If you want to take part, picture plush carpets
in his favorite room and sets of antlers mounted
next to portraits of his father and himself. Know
you are only a few decimal points from being me.
The waste in his pipe, his very own waste, well,
you might say I've liberated it, let it out.
My plan is to be sitting in his chair when he returns
from where he'll have found himself knee deep.
If you want to be part of this, perhaps bring a friend.
I'll meet you in the garden where I wait without shoes.
Who knows what we'll do when his room is ours.

OCTOBER, 2008

LITTLE GOOD SONG

It's good to sneak up from behind
to the front, good to sit
for a while in the best seats.
When the rich show up it's good
to explain how they're mistaken,
and cite the small, unreadable print.
The meek are ready, you tell them it says,
the meek have come to take their seats.

In my dream I'm addressing a large class
about Trotsky and Rimbaud. Trotsky
wanted perpetual revolution, I tell them,
Rimbaud a derangement of the senses.
Wouldn't it be fun to have dinner with them?

Most of my students have forsaken home,
or are planning to. They don't want
to have dinner with anybody.
They've mastered the boredom
they think conceals them. But the hungers

of the few are palpable, they're famished
for the marrow of experience, for the yet
to arrive viscera of their historical moment.
Rimbaud is now twenty-two, I say,
gunrunning in Africa. He's already given up

poetry, grown tired of breaking its rules.
Trotsky has fled to Mexico. Stalin's thugs
will soon cross the border with their ice axes.
My class is called Whatever I Feel Like
Talking About. No matter what the subject,

over the years it's been the only course
I've ever taught. Meanwhile, a rose explodes
on the chalkboard, three crows caw a hole

in the sky. My job is to shatter a few things.
Should I put them back together?

What's going on here? What kind of dream
with Rimbaud in it finds itself concerned
with responsibility? Yet I ask,
What's the responsibility of the lyric poet?
How it feels being himself? Why should

anyone care? And the political philosopher,
shouldn't he know a wildness can't go on forever?
Perpetual anything, I say, give me a break.
Just how many deaths can a good idea justify?
This dream is in need of a boutonniere,

or maybe a bullet suspended in midair.
But just in time a student rises and says,
In the spirit of Trotsky, let's tear up
all our notes from this class-ridden class,
let's caress the world with leaflets.

Half of the class follows him out the door.
Clearly, I've poorly educated the others
who remain seated, terrified they can't find
what's next on the syllabus.
But there, isolated among them, is that boy,

my Rimbaudian, all testosterone and refusal,
the one I always teach to, look how
he shrugs and heads toward the exit
as if the future already had assured him
it has openings for someone so unafraid of it,

his assignments unfinished, his grade in doubt.

THE MELANCHOLY OF THE EXTRATERRESTRIALS

Most of us who have insinuated ourselves
into their workdays and country clubs
come home at night and immediately take out

our little radios, and report to the mother ship
that our accents had been perfect, our manners
seamless and undetectable. I, for one, have lived

for such praise. We'd look at each other,
honored to be serving our planet, then break
out a bottle of something, and toast to seats

on school boards, and to those future sinecures
of leverage in local government. To what end?
That was only hinted at. Blend in, the elders told us,

be effective. When history becomes a subject
at any gathering, remember to have sympathy
for the Indians, mild disapproval for the colonists,

and do try to be neutral whenever the talk turns
to outer space. It was good advice, but the cost
of our achievements began to show on our faces.

After a while, I'd bring home a weariness,
and when I'd look in the mirror I'd see a creature
made of smoke and pretense, losing desire

to please the mother ship, which had begun—
all of us felt this—to take us for granted.
Why were we doing what we were doing?

Last week one of the humans invited me
to meet his wife and children. I've begun to fear
that soon I might be asked to break into that stash

of electro-atomic weaponry we were given,
and do something otherworldly to these people
who, in spite of their relative lack of culture

and intelligence, have shown me such kindness.
They are guilty, I see now, only of being born
on the wrong planet at a time of our ascendancy.

ONCE UPON

None of us thought anything of it
until one day we did.

The rectangular room has four blue walls,
the octagonal room four blue,
four cream, and the chairs in each
were built to fit Mister just right,

though he mostly chooses to lie
on that divan he won't call a couch.
He refers to the dining room
as the trapezoidal room, and says

we must, too, though to us it looks
square, and if truth be further told,
it's beige, though the Missus
says it's mocha,

she who once insisted flesh color
is a very nice shade of white.
She said this to Saher, the Indian girl
who manicures her nails.

None of us thought anything of it
until one day we did.

The circular room is the playroom
where the children go round and around.

We pick up their toys and scrub
the crayoned walls

after they're tired and go to bed.
And when the owners go to bed
we gather in our sleeping quarters
with our guitars.

That's where the songs got started,
and the words got found
for what we didn't know we thought.
Soon something is going to happen.

We think about it all the time.

Our good friends are with us, Jack and Jen,
old lefties with whom we now and then share
what we don't call our wealth. We clink our
wineglasses, and I say, Let's drink to privilege . . .

the privilege of evenings like this.
All our words have a radical past, and Jack
is famous for wanting the cog to fit the wheel,
and for the wheel to go straight

down some good-cause road. But he says
No, let's drink to an evening as solemn
as Eugene Debs demanding fair wages—
his smile the bent arrow only the best men

can point at themselves. I serve the salad
Barbara has made with pine nuts, fennel,
and fine, stinky cheese. It's too beautiful to eat,
Jen says, but means it only as a compliment.

Over the years she's eaten the beautiful
and accommodated mixed feelings, walked
through squalor as often as the rest of us
to reach some golden center of a city.

Here's to an evening of contradictions,
I say, let's never live without them.
We're in northern Appalachia
where strip mining and slag heaps

uglify the nearby mountains, and where
the already poor will lose their jobs
if the ugliness is corrected.
A sign on the interstate says Noah's Ark

Being Rebuilt Here. Here is where irony
dies its regular public death, and many believe
they're telling the truth
by simply saying what they think,

which means *here* is like most places.
Jack's about to say something, but the scallops
dappled with sesame seeds and wrapped in bacon
are ready. They're especially delicious,

Barbara says, because they're unnecessary.
Our friends don't seem to think that's funny,
but we all dig in to the unnecessary as if
we can't get enough of it. As I was about to say,

Jack says, ever since Obama, I'm feeling
a widespread sense of decency, aren't all of you?
I'd like to agree with him, but widespread
suddenly makes me think of the night sky

and large, empty spaces. More like pinpricks
of decency, I want to say, isolated little outposts,
but here comes Barbara with the shameless
store-bought cheesecake called Strawberry Swirl,

which, for a while, tends to end all arguments,
though there was a time we'd have renounced it—
back then when evenings like this were emblems
of excess and vapidity and a life that made us furious.

Though we should not speak about the soul,
that is, about things we don't know,
I'm sure mine sleeps the day long,
waiting to be jolted, even jilted awake,
preferably by joy, but also has been stirred
when sadness comes with a few of its songs.

And because no one landscape compels me,
except the one that's always out of reach
(toward which, nightly, I go), I find myself
conjuring Breugel-like peasants cavorting
under a Magritte-like sky—a landscape,
I think, the soul if fully awake might love.

But the soul is rumored to desire a room,
a chamber, really, in some faraway outpost
of the heart. Landscape can be lonely and cold.
Be sweet to me, world.

IV

DISCREPANCIES

It has something to do with ugliness,
even more, perhaps, with aggression,
but horseflies inspire no affection,
even though they're superb pilots.

Maybe because once they were squirmy,
furry things, butterflies seem content
with their sudden beauty, no interest
in getting anywhere fast.

The small brown bird outside my window
has a lilt and a tune. Elsewhere, a baby
is screeching. Watch out, little ones,
there are hawks, there are sleep-deprived

parents, utterly beside themselves.
When I was a child I claimed a grasshopper
hopped over a rock like a rockhopper.
"He likes to play with language," my mother

told her friends, "he's so smart."
She used to hide money in a coffee can,
place it behind the wooden matches
in the cupboard. I swear I never stole it.

She was beautiful, as was our neighbor
with the red jewel on her forehead.
That there's so little justice in the world—
one of them believed, the other experienced.

To ants a sparrow might as well be
a pterodactyl, and a parrot just one more
bright enormity to ignore
as they go about their business. I've tried

to become someone else for a while,
only to discover that he, too, was me.
I think I must learn to scrunch down
to the size of the smallest thing.

BAD

My wife is working in her room,
writing, and I've come in three times
with idle chatter, some not-new news.
The fourth time she identifies me
as what I am, a man lost
in late afternoon, in the terrible
in between—good work long over,
a good drink not yet
what the clock has okayed.
Her mood: a little bemused—
leave-me-the-hell-alone
mixed with a weary smile,
and I see my face
up on the Post Office wall
among Men Least Wanted,
looking forlorn. In the small print
under my name: *Annoying*
to loved ones in the afternoons,
lacks inner resources.
I go away, guilty as charged,
and write this poem, which I insist
she read at drinking time.
She's reading it now. It seems
she's pleased, but when she speaks
it's about charm, and how predictable
I am—how, when in trouble
I try to become irresistible
like one of those blond dogs

with a red bandanna around his neck,
sorry he's peed on the rug.
Forget it, she says, this stuff
is old, it won't work anymore,
and I hear Good boy, Good boy,
and can't stop licking her hand.

CONNUBIAL

Because with alarming accuracy
she'd been identifying patterns
I was unaware of—this tic, that
tendency, like the way I've mastered
the language of intimacy
in order to conceal how I felt—

I knew I was in danger
of being terribly understood.

If the imagined woman makes the real woman
seem bare-boned, hardly existent, lacking in
gracefulnesss and intellect and pulchritude,
and if you come to realize the imagined woman
can only satisfy your imagination, whereas
the real woman with all her limitations
can often make you feel good, how, in spite
of knowing this, does the imagined woman
keep getting into your bedroom, and joining you
at dinner, why is it that you always bring her along
on vacations when the real woman is shopping,
or figuring the best way to the museum?

                    And if the real woman

has an imagined man, as she must, someone
probably with her at this very moment, in fact
doing and saying everything she's ever wanted,
would you want to know that he slips in
to her life every day from a secret doorway
she's made for him, that he's present even when
you're eating your omelette at breakfast,
or do you prefer how she goes about the house
as she does, as if there were just the two of you?
Isn't her silence, finally, loving? And yours
not entirely self-serving? Hasn't the time come,

              once again, not to talk about it?

The experts were at work doing expert work.
Amateurs were loving what they hardly knew.
Houston, Tranquility Base here, the Eagle
has landed—came over our televisions,
accidental poetry, instant lore.
Our parents couldn't believe it.
Can you believe it? said my sister Sam.
Elsewhere on terra firma, a chemist
must have smiled an inner smile,
having perfected Agent Orange.
Mistakes were made, said our president;
nary a personal pronoun could be heard.
My friend on acid said he was the bullet,
but sometimes also the wound. The moon
was finished, he went on to explain,
never again would haunt or beguile.
Mary Travers was leaving on a jet plane,
didn't know when she'd be back again;
I, for one, was sad. Soon everyone
had a harmonica. On every street corner,
a guitar. A few of us thought we thought
it was possible to change the world.
We were love's amateurs, its happy fools.
I let my hair grow into a badge,
became an expert on right and wrong,
and under artificial light in my room,
read strangely comforting books
about alienation and despair. Meanwhile,

almost unnoticed, quotation marks
descended from the sky, began to fit
around everything we thought we knew.
And trod upon or not, the obstinate moon
would only be itself, kept bumping up
the crime rate, lifting the helpless seas.

ON THE PRAIRIE

Because I'd come from the east
where many believed
the land beyond the Hudson
squeezed into inconsequence,
as it did on Steinberg's map,

it took a while to appreciate
the beauty of vast spaces
and the occasional cluster
of cottonwoods sheltering
a farmhouse from the wind,

even longer to understand
the importance of a good silo,
and the way decency
and its intolerant twin, rectitude,
did battle in home after home.

I had strolled Fifth Avenue
in springtime, was accustomed
to women with a knack
for being seen. Most women
on the prairie dressed down,

didn't try to elevate themselves
with uncomfortable shoes,
and on principle, it seemed,
didn't sway when they walked.

Soon I was seeing beauty
in healthiness and big bones,
and in a manner of welcoming
that could lead a man
to think of progeny, if not ruin.

I learned to talk dirt with farmers,
play poker with men who spoke
John Deere, well practiced
at what was prudent to conceal.
Everyone I met seemed to know
what I needed to lose.

LANDSCAPE WITH FRIENDS

Impatient with but careful of life's hazards,
and in regular negotiations with courage,
there, ahead of me, I'd see a landscape,
say, meadow grass with patches of bluebells,
in other words a facade, and beyond it
would be a forest also with its concealments,
which I'd feel no need to investigate.
It was pleasure enough to have read about
all those animals and insects and their
acceptable murders and subterranean labors,
and how the trees and flowers nicely cover
it all up, leaving what we call beauty.

And though I admired those whose breadth
of fascination included the just-found path,
traces of deer scat, or sudden flourishes
of bright color in swampland, I would stay put
on the edges while they went in. And when
they'd return, fresh faced, without any
nonsense about bettering their souls, I'd praise
how undaunted they'd been by the prospect
of ticks and those spiders that watch
from the sticky architecture of their webs.

And they in turn would allow me my distance
because, after all, we were friends, each of us
quite sure, after many mistakes and infringements,
a person's pleasure must be his own serious business.

You're not surprised that you weren't surprised
by how insufficient it all felt—the lovely
kaleidoscopic violence of the Northern Lights

one night in Maine, or, say, that hummingbird's
demonic display of metabolism in your garden.
By then, many a beautiful strangeness
had come your way, leaving you enthralled,

or impelled to imagine another world,
or how it might feel to hover
athletically over the things you love.

It was no different than the day
you slanged a few words into consequence,
and later heard a mandolin so finely played
it made you weep. Each time

you felt something more was needed
if a great celebration were to begin.

There was so much docility you hadn't
yet disturbed, so much bafflement
in the face of a hundred things
it seemed important to understand.

Cacophony, a clink or clank, perhaps
some broad, unnerving, guttural claim—

you hadn't tried half the ways
to shake loose what's buried and large.

But even if you had, to shake loose
is not to have or to own. You've learned
not to send invitations out too soon.

Of course there've been times
you've not needed an occasion to break out
the Dom Pérignon, and times you've been able

to toast yourself for being one of those men
who can be beaten but hard to defeat.
You know all about taking small sips

for small reasons. As now, before dinner,
in your garden with your fluted glass
more than half full, and the last splinter
of dusk's light refracting from its rim,

you feel you've been given a gift, a moment
to seize and name—and sweet though it is,
hardly enough for a great celebration to begin.

FINAL BOW

In my sleep last night
when the small world of everyone
who's ever mattered in my life
showed up to help me die,
I mustered the strength

to rise and bow to them—
a conductor's bow, that deep
bending at the waist, right arm
across my stomach,
the left behind my back.

At first it seemed like the comedy
of aging had revised an old scene—
how, with time running out,
I'd make the winning shot
in my schoolyard of dreams,

only now I was wearing
an unheroic hospital gown,
apparently willing to look foolish—
for what? what no longer mattered?—
before I lay again down.

A House, a Desk, and a Chair

Really, you have no choice,
but you'll believe that you do.
We build that error in.
As we also do the notion of hope.
One of us, this very moment,
in beautifully formed cursive,
is misspelling who you are.
You are what we consider fun.

It seems normal, doesn't it—
your house, your desk, your chair.
But you, like the others,
have been assigned arbitrary places
in our world. We have supplied
and will continue to supply you
with all the illusions a man needs
to stay exactly where he is,

and you will call it destiny,
you will call it the place
you've worked so hard to achieve.
In fact, you'll feel unscripted,
and it does not matter
that you're learning this now.
The script says you'll forget.

You are programmed to worship us,
who are kind, ethereal, perfect.

You kneel to ask our blessings,
and find reasons for our silence.
No matter what we do, we're sure
that even now you're saying
to yourself: *kind, ethereal, perfect,*
that the three have become one.

If you find yourself in the elsewhere of an evening,
leaning against the wall at a party, hoping someone
who remembers Brando or Montgomery Clift would
find your *come join me in a life of alienation* pose
attractive, isn't it true that even the people your age
are thinking, Oh there's an old man leaning against
a wall, poor soul, he must be lonely or bored?

But if you're also the kind of man who can't stop playing
movies in his head, and still believes
he's capable of being a major character
in his own shenanigans, well, maybe, what the hell,
time to risk being a public fool. Maybe that woman
standing by the wet bar, so nicely in the middle ground
between young and old, in what looks like a shirt

with buttons open clear to her waist . . . no, she's not
really looking your way. But if she were, if she had
any sense, if she shared a nostalgia for what happened
in a slower, everything-at-stake world, or envied, say,
Ingrid Bergman, gorgeous with grief, in need of
being consoled—wouldn't she now make a gesture
to someone like you, who might understand

the twenty-three varieties of despair? Certainly,
you're thinking, as you lean back against the wall,
experience is on your side. Which means you might
want to give her what she doesn't know she wants.

What good are movies for? Isn't it time to display
how far back your knowledge goes, your Jimmy Stewart
boyish enthusiasms, your big, indestructible heart?

To My Doppelganger

You were always the careful one,
who'd tiptoe into passion
and cut it in half with your mind.
I allowed you that, and went
happier, wilder ways. Now
every thought I've ever had
seems a rope knotted
to another rope, going back
in time. We're intertwined.
I've learned to hesitate
before even the most open door.
I don't know what you've learned.
But to go forward, I feel,
is to go together now. There's a place
I'd like to arrive by nightfall.